Keto for Cancer

Cookbook

A New Unique way to approach cancer by Ketogenic Diet Recipes for Cancer treatments and management.

Dr. Jemy Cole

Copyright © 2023 by Dr. Jemy Cole

All rights reserved.

No part of this publication may be reproduced, distributed, or transmitted in any form or by any means, including photocopying, recording, or other electronic or mechanical methods, without the prior written permission of the publisher, except in the case of brief quotations embodied in critical reviews and certain other noncommercial uses permitted by copyright law.

TABLE OF CONTENTS

Introduction 4

Understanding the ketogenic diet 6

Benefits of a ketogenic diet for cancer patients .. 8

Important considerations for cancer patients on keto 10

Chapter 2: Breakfast Recipes 12

Chapter 3: Lunch Recipes 29

Chapter 4: Dinner Recipes 49

Chapter 5: Snack Recipes 72

Chapter 6: Dessert Recipes 89

Chapter 7: Tips and Tricks for Success 108

Meal prep ideas 109

Grocery shopping for keto ingredients 110

Storing and reheating meals 112

Eating out on keto 114

Chapter 8: Conclusion 116

The importance of a balanced diet during cancer treatment 116

Final thoughts on the ketogenic diet and cancer 118

Introduction

John had just received his cancer diagnosis, and he was feeling overwhelmed and scared. Like many cancer patients, he was worried about the side effects of his treatments and how they would impact his overall health and wellbeing. John knew he needed to take control of his health, and that's when he stumbled upon the ketogenic diet.

After reading up on the ketogenic diet and its benefits for cancer patients, John started to feel hopeful. He began researching and experimenting with different keto recipes, but he found that many of them were not suited for his unique needs as a cancer patient.

That's when John discovered my Keto for Cancer Recipes Cookbook. As he flipped through the pages, he was excited to find a wide variety of delicious and nutritious keto recipes that were specifically designed for cancer patients. He appreciated how the cookbook provided detailed nutritional information for each recipe, which gave him confidence that he was making the best choices for his health.

As John started incorporating these recipes into his diet, he noticed a significant improvement in his overall wellbeing.

He had more energy, felt less fatigued, and experienced fewer side effects from his treatments. John's journey inspired me to write this cookbook, with the hope of providing cancer patients with a valuable resource to help them feel empowered and confident in their journey towards better health.

In this Keto for Cancer Recipes Cookbook, I'll guide you through the basics of the ketogenic diet, and share with you the benefits that it can offer to cancer patients. You'll find a wide range of delicious and easy-to-prepare recipes that are designed to support your body's nutritional needs during this challenging time.

Whether you're new to the ketogenic diet or have been following it for a while, this cookbook has something for everyone. From breakfast to dessert, you'll find recipes that are not only delicious but also packed with the nutrients your body needs to heal and thrive.

Throughout this cookbook, you'll find tips and tricks for success, including meal prep ideas, grocery shopping tips, and advice on how to eat out while staying on track with your keto diet. My hope is that this cookbook will serve as a valuable resource for you, providing you with the tools and information you need to take control of your health and wellbeing during your cancer journey.

So, let's get started on this journey towards better health together. Together, we can empower ourselves and our loved ones to live our best lives, even in the face of cancer.

Understanding the ketogenic diet

The ketogenic diet, or keto for short, is a low-carbohydrate, high-fat diet that has been gaining popularity in recent years for its potential health benefits, including weight loss, improved blood sugar control, and even some evidence of anti-cancer effects.

The basic principle of the ketogenic diet is to switch the body's primary source of fuel from glucose (which comes from carbohydrates) to ketones (which are produced by the liver when the body is in a state of ketosis). To achieve this state, the keto diet typically limits carbohydrate intake to less than 50 grams per day, while increasing fat intake to around 70-80% of total calories.

By restricting carbohydrates, the body is forced to break down stored fat into ketones, which are then used as an energy source instead of glucose. This process can help to lower blood sugar and insulin levels, and may even have some anti-inflammatory and anti-cancer effects.

While the ketogenic diet has gained popularity in recent years, it's important to note that it may not be suitable for everyone. Individuals with certain medical conditions, such as pancreatitis, liver disease, or gallbladder disease, may need to avoid the keto diet or consult with a healthcare provider before starting it. Additionally, some people may experience side effects such as constipation, fatigue, or nutrient deficiencies if they do not follow the diet properly.

Overall, the ketogenic diet has potential health benefits for some individuals, including cancer patients. However, it's important to understand the principles of the diet and consult with a healthcare provider before starting it to ensure that it is safe and appropriate for your individual needs.

Benefits of a ketogenic diet for cancer patients

While research on the effects of the ketogenic diet on cancer is still in its early stages, there is growing evidence that suggests the diet may offer some benefits for cancer patients.

Here are a few potential benefits of a ketogenic diet for cancer patients:

Reduced glucose availability: Cancer cells rely heavily on glucose for their energy needs, and the ketogenic diet restricts glucose availability in the body. This may help to starve cancer cells of their primary energy source and slow their growth.

Reduced inflammation: The ketogenic diet has been shown to reduce inflammation in the body, which is a key factor in the development and progression of many chronic diseases, including cancer.

Enhanced immune function: Some studies suggest that the ketogenic diet may enhance immune function, which could help the body to better fight cancer cells.

Improved metabolic health: The ketogenic diet has been shown to improve metabolic health markers, such as blood sugar and insulin levels, which may be beneficial for cancer patients who often experience metabolic disturbances.

Weight loss: The ketogenic diet may promote weight loss, which can be important for cancer patients who may experience weight gain as a result of their treatments. Maintaining a healthy weight can also improve overall health outcomes and reduce the risk of cancer recurrence.

It's important to note that the ketogenic diet should not be seen as a standalone treatment for cancer. Rather, it should be used as part of a comprehensive cancer treatment plan that is tailored to the individual patient's needs. Cancer patients considering a ketogenic diet should consult with a healthcare provider before starting it to ensure that it is safe and appropriate for their individual needs.

Important considerations for cancer patients on keto

While the ketogenic diet may offer some benefits for cancer patients, there are also some important considerations that should be taken into account when considering this diet.

Here are a few key factors to keep in mind:

Nutrient deficiencies: The ketogenic diet can be low in certain nutrients, such as fiber, vitamin C, and potassium. Cancer patients who are already at risk for nutrient deficiencies due to their disease or treatment may need to take extra precautions to ensure that they are getting all the nutrients they need.

Energy levels: The ketogenic diet can be difficult to sustain in the long term and may cause some people to experience fatigue or weakness. Cancer patients who are already dealing with fatigue or other symptoms may find the diet to be too challenging.

Medications: Cancer patients who are taking medications should consult with their healthcare provider before starting the ketogenic diet, as it may interact with some medications and affect their efficacy.

Personal preferences: The ketogenic diet may not be suitable for everyone and some people may find it difficult to adhere to. Cancer patients who are already dealing with a lot of stress and anxiety may find the diet to be too challenging.

Monitoring: Cancer patients who are on the ketogenic diet should be closely monitored by a healthcare provider to ensure that they are not experiencing any adverse effects, such as nutrient deficiencies or electrolyte imbalances.

the ketogenic diet may be a viable option for some cancer patients, but it's important to consider all the potential risks and benefits before making a decision. Cancer patients should work with their healthcare provider to develop a comprehensive treatment plan that takes into account their individual needs and preferences.

Chapter 2: Breakfast Recipes

Chapter 2 of the Keto for Cancer Recipes Cookbook focuses on breakfast recipes that are suitable for a ketogenic diet. These recipes are designed to provide cancer patients with a nourishing and satisfying start to their day while also adhering to the principles of a low-carbohydrate, high-fat diet. From hearty omelets filled with vegetables and cheese to sweet and satisfying chia seed puddings, these recipes offer a range of flavors and textures to suit any palate. Whether you're looking for a quick and easy breakfast that can be made in minutes or a more elaborate brunch dish to enjoy on the weekends, this chapter has something for everyone.

Keto breakfast bowl with vegetables and eggs

Ingredients:

2 cups chopped vegetables (such as spinach, kale, bell peppers, and mushrooms)

2 tbsp olive oil

4 large eggs

1 avocado, sliced

Salt and pepper, to taste

Instructions:

Heat the olive oil in a large skillet over medium heat. Add the chopped vegetables and sauté until tender, about 5-7 minutes.

While the vegetables are cooking, crack the eggs into a bowl and whisk until well beaten. Season with salt and pepper.

Once the vegetables are cooked, push them to one side of the skillet and pour the beaten eggs into the other side. Cook until the eggs are set, about 2-3 minutes.

Divide the vegetable and egg mixture between two bowls. Top each bowl with sliced avocado and additional salt and pepper, if desired.

This keto breakfast bowl is high in fiber, healthy fats, and protein, making it a great option for cancer patients who want to start their day off on the right foot. It's also easy to customize with your favorite vegetables and seasonings, so feel free to experiment and make it your own!

Keto coconut flour pancakes

Ingredients:

1/4 cup coconut flour

1/4 tsp baking powder

1/4 tsp salt

1/4 tsp cinnamon (optional)

3 large eggs

1/4 cup unsweetened almond milk

2 tbsp coconut oil, melted

1 tsp vanilla extract

Instructions:

In a mixing bowl, whisk together the coconut flour, baking powder, salt, and cinnamon (if using).

In a separate bowl, whisk together the eggs, almond milk, melted coconut oil, and vanilla extract.

Pour the wet ingredients into the dry ingredients and whisk until well combined.

Heat a non-stick skillet or griddle over medium heat. Grease with cooking spray or additional coconut oil.

Pour 1/4 cup of the pancake batter onto the skillet for each pancake. Cook for 2-3 minutes, or until bubbles begin to form on the surface. Flip and cook for an additional 1-2 minutes on the other side.

Repeat with the remaining batter, adding more coconut oil to the skillet as needed.

Serve the pancakes warm with your favorite low-carbohydrate toppings, such as butter, sugar-free syrup, or fresh berries.

These keto coconut flour pancakes are fluffy, flavorful, and perfect for satisfying your pancake cravings while still adhering to a low-carbohydrate, high-fat diet. They're also high in fiber and healthy fats, making them a filling and nutritious breakfast option for cancer patients.

Avocado and egg salad

Ingredients:

2 hard-boiled eggs, peeled and chopped

1 ripe avocado, peeled and chopped

1 small tomato, chopped

1/4 cup chopped red onion

1 tbsp chopped fresh cilantro

Juice of 1/2 lime

Salt and pepper, to taste

Instructions:

In a mixing bowl, combine the chopped eggs, avocado, tomato, red onion, and cilantro.

Drizzle the lime juice over the mixture and season with salt and pepper, to taste.

Gently toss the ingredients until well combined.

Serve the avocado and egg salad immediately, either on its own or with a side of low-carbohydrate crackers or bread.

This avocado and egg salad is high in healthy fats and protein, making it a satisfying and nutritious breakfast option for cancer patients following a ketogenic diet. It's also easy to customize with your favorite herbs and spices, so feel free to experiment and make it your own!

Keto breakfast smoothie

Ingredients:

1/2 cup unsweetened almond milk

1/2 cup full-fat Greek yogurt

1/2 avocado

1/2 cup frozen berries (such as strawberries, blueberries, or raspberries)

1 scoop vanilla whey protein powder

1 tbsp chia seeds

1 tbsp almond butter

1/4 tsp vanilla extract

Optional: sweetener of your choice (such as stevia or erythritol), to taste

Instructions:

Combine all of the ingredients in a blender and blend until smooth and creamy.

If the smoothie is too thick, add additional almond milk until it reaches your desired consistency.

Taste and adjust the sweetener, if desired.

Serve the keto breakfast smoothie immediately, garnished with fresh berries or a sprinkle of chia seeds, if desired.

Avocado and Bacon Breakfast Bowl:

Ingredients:

- 1 ripe avocado
- 2 strips of cooked bacon
- 2 eggs

- Salt and pepper to taste

Instructions:

Cut the avocado in half and remove the pit.

Scoop out a little flesh from each half to create space for the eggs.

Place the avocado halves in a baking dish.

Crack an egg into each avocado half.

Season with salt and pepper.

Bake at 350°F (175°C) for about 12-15 minutes or until the eggs are cooked to your liking.

Crumble the cooked bacon on top before serving.

Veggie and Cheese Omelette:

Ingredients:

- 3 eggs
- 1/4 cup diced bell peppers
- 1/4 cup diced onions
- 1/4 cup shredded cheddar cheese

- Salt and pepper to taste
- Butter or oil for cooking

Instructions:

In a bowl, whisk the eggs until well combined.

Heat butter or oil in a non-stick skillet over medium heat.

Add the diced bell peppers and onions to the skillet and sauté until they're tender.

Pour the whisked eggs over the veggies and let them cook for a minute.

Sprinkle shredded cheddar cheese over one half of the omelette.

Fold the other half over the cheese and cook until the eggs are fully set.

Slide the omelette onto a plate and season with salt and pepper.

Smoked Salmon Breakfast Wrap:

Ingredients:

- 2 large lettuce leaves (such as iceberg or romaine)

- 2 oz smoked salmon
- 2 tbsp cream cheese
- 1/4 avocado, sliced
- Fresh dill (optional)

Instructions:

1. Lay the lettuce leaves on a flat surface.
2. Spread a tablespoon of cream cheese onto each lettuce leaf.
3. Place the smoked salmon and avocado slices on top of the cream cheese.
4. Sprinkle with fresh dill if desired.
5. Roll up the lettuce leaves like a wrap and secure with toothpicks if needed.

Keto Greek Yogurt Parfait:

Ingredients:

- 1/2 cup full-fat Greek yogurt
- 1/4 cup mixed berries (blueberries, raspberries, strawberries)

- 2 tbsp chopped nuts (almonds, walnuts, or pecans)
- 1 tsp chia seeds
- 1 tsp honey (optional)

Instructions:

In a glass or bowl, layer Greek yogurt, mixed berries, chopped nuts, and chia seeds.

Drizzle with a little honey if desired.

Repeat the layers if making multiple servings.

Serve immediately.

Coconut Chia Pudding:

Ingredients:

- 1/4 cup chia seeds
- 1 cup unsweetened coconut milk
- 1/2 tsp vanilla extract
- 1/4 cup unsweetened shredded coconut
- Low-carb sweetener to taste (stevia, erythritol, or monk fruit)

Instructions:

In a bowl, mix chia seeds, coconut milk, vanilla extract, and sweetener.

Stir well and let it sit for about 15 minutes, stirring occasionally to prevent clumping.

Stir in shredded coconut.

Cover and refrigerate overnight.

Serve with additional coconut flakes on top.

Spinach and Feta Breakfast Casserole: Ingredients:
- 4 cups baby spinach
- 1/2 cup crumbled feta cheese
- 8 eggs
- 1/4 cup heavy cream
- Salt and pepper to taste
- Butter or oil for greasing

Instructions:

Preheat the oven to 350°F (175°C) and grease a baking dish.

Sauté the baby spinach in a pan until wilted.

Spread the wilted spinach evenly in the baking dish.

Sprinkle crumbled feta cheese over the spinach.

In a bowl, whisk together eggs, heavy cream, salt, and pepper.

Pour the egg mixture over the spinach and feta.

Bake for about 25-30 minutes or until the eggs are set.

Allow the casserole to cool slightly before slicing and serving.

Keto Breakfast Smoothie:

Ingredients:

- 1 cup unsweetened almond milk
- 1/4 cup frozen berries (blueberries, raspberries, strawberries)
- 1 tbsp almond butter
- 1 scoop of low-carb protein powder
- 1 tbsp chia seeds

Instructions:

In a blender, combine almond milk, frozen berries, almond butter, protein powder, and chia seeds.

Blend until smooth and creamy.

Add ice if desired for a thicker texture.

Pour into a glass and enjoy.

Zucchini and Cheese Muffins:

Ingredients:

- 2 cups grated zucchini
- 1 cup almond flour
- 1/2 cup grated Parmesan cheese
- 1/4 cup chopped fresh herbs (such as parsley and chives)
- 3 eggs
- 1/4 cup melted butter
- 1 tsp baking powder
- Salt and pepper to taste

Instructions:

Preheat the oven to 350°F (175°C) and line a muffin tin with paper liners.

In a bowl, combine grated zucchini, almond flour, grated Parmesan cheese, and chopped herbs.

In a separate bowl, whisk together eggs, melted butter, baking powder, salt, and pepper.

Mix the wet and dry ingredients until well combined.

Divide the batter evenly among the muffin cups.

Bake for about 20-25 minutes or until the muffins are golden and a toothpick inserted into the center comes out clean.

Keto Breakfast Burrito:

Ingredients:

- 2 large eggs
- 2 slices cooked bacon, crumbled
- 1/4 avocado, sliced
- 2 tbsp shredded cheddar cheese
- 1 low-carb tortilla

Instructions:

Scramble the eggs in a pan until cooked to your liking.

Lay the low-carb tortilla flat on a plate.

Place the scrambled eggs, crumbled bacon, avocado slices, and shredded cheddar cheese in the center of the tortilla.

Fold in the sides of the tortilla and then roll it up into a burrito.

Chia Seed Breakfast Bowl:

Ingredients:

- 3 tbsp chia seeds
- 1 cup unsweetened almond milk
- 1/4 cup chopped nuts (almonds, walnuts, or pecans)
- 1/4 cup diced low-carb fruits (such as berries)
- Cinnamon and nutmeg to taste

Instructions:

Mix chia seeds and almond milk in a bowl.

Stir well and let it sit for about 10-15 minutes, stirring occasionally to prevent clumping.

Top with chopped nuts, diced fruits, and a sprinkle of cinnamon and nutmeg.

Mix everything together and enjoy.

Remember that these recipes are designed to be keto-friendly and include ingredients that are generally considered low in carbohydrates and suitable for a ketogenic diet. However, individual dietary needs may vary, especially for individuals with specific health conditions such as cancer. It's always a good idea to consult with a healthcare professional or registered dietitian before making significant changes to your diet, especially if you have health concerns.

Chapter 3: Lunch Recipes

Lunch is an important meal of the day that provides the necessary energy and nutrients to get through the rest of the day. For cancer patients following a ketogenic diet, it's essential to choose low-carbohydrate, high-fat options that support their health and well-being. In this chapter, we'll explore a variety of delicious and nutritious lunch recipes that are perfect for cancer patients on keto, from hearty salads to comforting soups and stews. These recipes are easy to prepare, easy to customize, and full of flavor, making them a great addition to any cancer patient's meal plan.

Grilled chicken Caesar salad with keto dressing

Ingredients:

For the salad:

2 boneless, skinless chicken breasts

Salt and pepper, to taste

6 cups chopped romaine lettuce

1/2 cup grated Parmesan cheese

1/2 cup crumbled bacon

Optional: chopped tomatoes, sliced avocado, or additional vegetables of your choice

For the dressing:

1/2 cup mayonnaise

1/4 cup grated Parmesan cheese

2 tbsp lemon juice

1 tbsp Dijon mustard

1 clove garlic, minced

Salt and pepper, to taste

Instructions:

Preheat a grill or grill pan over medium-high heat. Season the chicken breasts with salt and pepper, to taste.

Grill the chicken for 5-6 minutes per side, or until cooked through. Set aside to cool.

In a mixing bowl, combine the romaine lettuce, Parmesan cheese, and bacon.

Slice the cooled chicken breasts and add them to the salad. If desired, add additional vegetables of your choice.

In a separate mixing bowl, whisk together the mayonnaise, Parmesan cheese, lemon juice, Dijon mustard, garlic, salt, and pepper.

Drizzle the dressing over the salad and toss until well combined.

Serve the grilled chicken Caesar salad immediately, garnished with additional Parmesan cheese or croutons, if desired.

This grilled chicken Caesar salad with keto dressing is high in protein and healthy fats, making it a filling and nutritious lunch option for cancer patients following a ketogenic diet. It's also easy to customize with your favorite low-carbohydrate vegetables and toppings, so feel free to make it your own!

Zucchini noodles with shrimp and pesto

Ingredients:

2 medium zucchini, spiralized or julienned into noodles

1/2 lb shrimp, peeled and deveined

1/4 cup pesto (homemade or store-bought)

2 tbsp olive oil

Salt and pepper, to taste

Optional: grated Parmesan cheese, cherry tomatoes, or additional vegetables of your choice

Instructions:

Heat the olive oil in a large skillet over medium-high heat.

Add the shrimp to the skillet and cook for 2-3 minutes per side, or until pink and cooked through. Remove from the skillet and set aside.

Add the zucchini noodles to the same skillet and cook for 1-2 minutes, or until tender.

Add the cooked shrimp and pesto to the skillet with the zucchini noodles. Toss until well combined.

Season with salt and pepper, to taste.

Serve the zucchini noodles with shrimp and pesto immediately, garnished with grated Parmesan cheese, cherry tomatoes, or additional vegetables of your choice, if desired.

This zucchini noodle dish with shrimp and pesto is a delicious and healthy lunch option for cancer patients following a ketogenic diet. The zucchini noodles provide a low-carbohydrate alternative to traditional pasta, and the shrimp and pesto provide plenty of healthy fats and protein to keep you satisfied throughout the day. Plus, it's easy to customize with your favorite vegetables and toppings, so feel free to get creative and make it your own!

Broccoli and cheese soup

Ingredients:

4 cups chopped broccoli florets

4 cups chicken or vegetable broth

1 cup heavy cream

1 cup shredded cheddar cheese

2 tbsp butter

2 cloves garlic, minced

Salt and pepper, to taste

Instructions:

In a large pot or Dutch oven, melt the butter over medium heat.

Add the minced garlic to the pot and cook for 1-2 minutes, or until fragrant.

Add the chopped broccoli florets to the pot and stir to combine.

Pour the chicken or vegetable broth into the pot and bring to a boil.

Reduce the heat to low and simmer for 10-15 minutes, or until the broccoli is tender.

Using an immersion blender or transferring the soup to a blender, blend the soup until smooth.

Add the heavy cream to the pot and stir until well combined.

Gradually add the shredded cheddar cheese to the pot, stirring until melted and fully incorporated.

Season with salt and pepper, to taste.

Serve the broccoli and cheese soup hot, garnished with additional shredded cheddar cheese or crumbled bacon, if desired.

This broccoli and cheese soup is a delicious and nutritious lunch option for cancer patients following a ketogenic diet. It's high in healthy fats and low in carbohydrates, making it a great choice for those looking to maintain their ketosis while still enjoying a comforting and satisfying meal. Plus, it's easy to customize with your favorite toppings and seasonings, so feel free to make it your own!

Bacon, lettuce, and tomato wrap with keto mayo

Ingredients:

4-6 large lettuce leaves (romaine or iceberg)

4-6 slices of cooked bacon

1-2 large tomatoes, sliced

Keto mayo (homemade or store-bought)

Salt and pepper, to taste

Instructions:

Wash and dry the lettuce leaves, and lay them out on a flat surface.

Spread a generous amount of keto mayo onto each lettuce leaf.

Place a slice of cooked bacon onto each lettuce leaf, followed by a few slices of tomato.

Season with salt and pepper, to taste.

Roll up each lettuce leaf tightly, tucking in the sides to create a wrap.

Serve the bacon, lettuce, and tomato wraps with keto mayo immediately, or wrap them in plastic wrap and store in the fridge for later.

This bacon, lettuce, and tomato wrap with keto mayo is a tasty and nutritious lunch option for cancer patients following a ketogenic diet. The lettuce leaves provide a low-carbohydrate alternative to traditional bread or wraps, while the bacon and mayo provide plenty of healthy fats and protein to keep you satisfied throughout the day. Plus, it's easy to customize with your favorite toppings and seasonings, so feel free to get creative and make it your own!

Grilled Chicken Salad

Ingredients:

- 2 boneless, skinless chicken breasts
- 4 cups mixed salad greens
- 1/4 cup sliced almonds
- 1/4 cup shredded Parmesan cheese
- 2 tbsp olive oil
- Salt and pepper to taste

Instructions:

Preheat a grill or grill pan over medium-high heat.

Season chicken breasts with salt and pepper. Grill for 6-8 minutes per side or until fully cooked.

Let the chicken rest for a few minutes, then slice it.

In a large bowl, toss the salad greens with olive oil and a pinch of salt.

Divide the salad greens among plates. Top with sliced chicken, almonds, and shredded Parmesan.

Zucchini Noodles with Pesto

Ingredients:

- 2 medium zucchinis, spiralized into noodles
- 1/2 cup homemade or store-bought pesto
- 1/4 cup cherry tomatoes, halved
- 2 tbsp pine nuts
- Salt and pepper to taste

Instructions:

Heat a large skillet over medium heat. Add pine nuts and toast until golden brown. Remove from skillet and set aside.

In the same skillet, add zucchini noodles and cook for 2-3 minutes until heated through.

Add pesto to the skillet and toss to coat the zucchini noodles.

Divide the zucchini noodles onto plates, and top with cherry tomatoes and toasted pine nuts.

Season with salt and pepper to taste.

Tuna Avocado Lettuce Wraps

Ingredients:

- 1 can (5 oz) tuna, drained
- 1 ripe avocado, diced
- 2 tbsp mayonnaise
- 1 tbsp Dijon mustard
- Lettuce leaves (such as Romaine or Butter lettuce)
- Salt and pepper to taste

Instructions:

In a bowl, mix tuna, diced avocado, mayonnaise, and Dijon mustard.

Season with salt and pepper to taste.

Place a spoonful of the tuna mixture onto each lettuce leaf.

Roll up the lettuce leaves to form wraps.

Serve as a handheld lunch option.

Cauliflower Fried Rice

Ingredients:

1 head cauliflower, riced (using a food processor or grater)

2 eggs, beaten

1 cup mixed vegetables (e.g., peas, carrots, bell peppers), diced

1/4 cup green onions, chopped

2 tbsp coconut aminos (or soy sauce if preferred)

2 tbsp coconut oil

Salt and pepper to taste

Instructions:

Heat coconut oil in a large skillet over medium heat.

Add diced vegetables to the skillet and sauté until slightly softened.

Push the vegetables to one side of the skillet and pour beaten eggs into the empty side. Scramble the eggs until cooked.

Combine the scrambled eggs with the vegetables, then add cauliflower rice to the skillet.

Pour coconut aminos over the mixture and stir-fry for 5-7 minutes, until the cauliflower rice is cooked and heated through.

Stir in chopped green onions and season with salt and pepper.

Serve as a flavorful alternative to traditional fried rice.

Salmon and Asparagus

Ingredients:

- 2 salmon fillets
- 1 bunch asparagus, trimmed
- 2 tbsp olive oil
- 2 cloves garlic, minced
- 1 lemon, sliced
- Salt and pepper to taste

Instructions:

Preheat the oven to 400°F (200°C).

Place salmon fillets on a baking sheet lined with parchment paper.

Arrange asparagus around the salmon on the baking sheet.

Drizzle olive oil over salmon and asparagus. Sprinkle minced garlic, salt, and pepper.

Place lemon slices on top of the salmon fillets.

Bake in the preheated oven for about 15-20 minutes, or until salmon flakes easily with a fork.

Serve with a squeeze of lemon juice.

Greek Salad with Chicken

Ingredients:

- 2 boneless, skinless chicken breasts
- 4 cups mixed salad greens
- 1/2 cup cherry tomatoes, halved
- 1/4 cup red onion, thinly sliced
- 1/4 cup Kalamata olives, pitted and halved

- 1/4 cup feta cheese, crumbled
- 2 tbsp olive oil
- 2 tbsp red wine vinegar
- 1 tsp dried oregano
- Salt and pepper to taste

Instructions:

Preheat a grill or grill pan over medium-high heat.

Season chicken breasts with dried oregano, salt, and pepper.

Grill for 6-8 minutes per side or until fully cooked.

Let the chicken rest for a few minutes, then slice it.

In a large bowl, combine salad greens, cherry tomatoes, red onion, Kalamata olives, and feta cheese.

In a small bowl, whisk together olive oil, red wine vinegar, salt, and pepper.

Drizzle the dressing over the salad and toss to combine.

Top the salad with sliced chicken.

Serve as a refreshing and satisfying lunch.

Egg Salad Lettuce Wraps

Ingredients:

- 4 hard-boiled eggs, chopped
- 1/4 cup mayonnaise
- 2 tsp Dijon mustard
- 2 green onions, chopped
- Salt and pepper to taste
- Lettuce leaves (such as Bibb or Iceberg)

Instructions:

In a bowl, mix chopped hard-boiled eggs, mayonnaise, Dijon mustard, chopped green onions, salt, and pepper.

Spoon the egg salad onto lettuce leaves.

Roll up the lettuce leaves to create wraps.

Enjoy as a light and flavorful lunch option.

Broccoli Cheese Soup

Ingredients:

- 2 cups broccoli florets
- 2 cups chicken or vegetable broth
- 1 cup heavy cream
- 1 cup shredded cheddar cheese
- 2 tbsp butter
- 1 small onion, chopped
- 2 cloves garlic, minced
- Salt and pepper to taste

Instructions:

In a large pot, melt butter over medium heat. Add chopped onion and minced garlic. Sauté until onion is translucent.

Add broccoli florets and sauté for another 2-3 minutes.

Pour in chicken or vegetable broth and bring to a simmer. Cook until broccoli is tender.

Use an immersion blender to blend the soup until smooth.

Stir in heavy cream and shredded cheddar cheese. Cook, stirring, until cheese is melted and the soup is heated through.

Season with salt and pepper to taste.

Serve warm as a comforting keto-friendly soup.

Caprese Salad with Pesto Chicken

Ingredients:

- 2 boneless, skinless chicken breasts
- 1/4 cup homemade or store-bought pesto
- 1 large tomato, sliced
- 1 ball fresh mozzarella cheese, sliced
- Fresh basil leaves
- Salt and pepper to taste

Instructions:

Preheat a grill or grill pan over medium-high heat.

Season chicken breasts with salt and pepper. Grill for 6-8 minutes per side or until fully cooked.

Let the chicken rest for a few minutes, then spread pesto over the chicken breasts.

On a serving platter, arrange tomato slices and fresh mozzarella slices.

Place the pesto-covered chicken breasts on top of the tomato and mozzarella slices.

Garnish with fresh basil leaves.

Drizzle with a touch of olive oil if desired.

Serve as a colorful and flavorful salad.

Cucumber and Avocado Soup

Ingredients:

- 2 cucumbers, peeled and chopped
- 1 ripe avocado, peeled and pitted
- 1 cup vegetable broth
- 1/2 cup fresh mint leaves
- 1/4 cup plain Greek yogurt
- 2 tbsp lemon juice

- Salt and pepper to taste

Instructions:

In a blender, combine chopped cucumbers, avocado, vegetable broth, mint leaves, Greek yogurt, and lemon juice.

Blend until smooth and creamy.

Season with salt and pepper to taste.

Chill the soup in the refrigerator for at least an hour before serving.

Serve cold as a refreshing summer soup.

Please keep in mind that these recipes are provided for informational purposes and should be adjusted to fit individual dietary preferences and needs. Additionally, make sure to consult with a healthcare professional before making significant dietary changes, especially during cancer treatment.

Chapter 4: Dinner Recipes

Dinner is an important meal of the day, and it's essential for cancer patients on a ketogenic diet to have nutritious and satisfying dinner options that help them maintain their ketosis while supporting their overall health. In this chapter, we'll explore a variety of dinner recipes that are high in healthy fats and protein, while low in carbohydrates. From hearty meat dishes to flavorful vegetarian options, these recipes are sure to satisfy your hunger and nourish your body.

Keto meatballs with zucchini noodles

Ingredients:

For the meatballs:

- 1 lb ground beef
- 1/2 cup almond flour
- 1 egg
- 2 cloves garlic, minced
- 1 tsp dried oregano
- 1 tsp dried basil
- 1/2 tsp salt

- 1/4 tsp black pepper
- For the zucchini noodles:
- 4 medium zucchinis, spiralized
- 2 tbsp olive oil
- Salt and pepper, to taste

Optional toppings:

- Keto-friendly marinara sauce
- Shredded Parmesan cheese
- Fresh parsley, chopped

Instructions:

Preheat the oven to 375°F.

In a large mixing bowl, combine the ground beef, almond flour, egg, minced garlic, dried oregano, dried basil, salt, and black pepper. Mix well until all ingredients are evenly combined.

Form the mixture into golf ball-sized meatballs and place them on a baking sheet lined with parchment paper.

Bake the meatballs in the preheated oven for 20-25 minutes, or until cooked through and golden brown.

While the meatballs are cooking, prepare the zucchini noodles. Heat the olive oil in a large skillet over medium-high heat. Add the zucchini noodles and season with salt and pepper, to taste. Cook for 3-4 minutes, or until tender.

Serve the meatballs on top of the zucchini noodles, and top with keto-friendly marinara sauce, shredded Parmesan cheese, and fresh parsley, if desired.

These keto meatballs with zucchini noodles are a flavorful and nutritious dinner option for cancer patients on a ketogenic diet. They're high in healthy fats and protein, while low in carbohydrates, making them a great choice for maintaining ketosis while nourishing your body. Plus, they're easy to customize with your favorite toppings and seasonings, so feel free to make them your own!

Keto chicken fajitas with cauliflower rice

Ingredients:

For the chicken fajitas:

- 1 lb boneless, skinless chicken breasts, sliced into thin strips
- 1 red bell pepper, sliced into thin strips
- 1 green bell pepper, sliced into thin strips
- 1/2 yellow onion, sliced into thin strips
- 2 tbsp olive oil
- 2 cloves garlic, minced
- 1 tsp chili powder
- 1 tsp cumin
- 1/2 tsp paprika
- Salt and pepper, to taste
- For the cauliflower rice:
- 1 head cauliflower, grated or riced
- 2 tbsp butter or ghee
- Salt and pepper, to taste

Optional toppings:

- Sliced avocado

- Shredded cheese
- Fresh cilantro, chopped

Instructions:

In a large mixing bowl, combine the chicken strips, sliced bell peppers, and sliced onion. Add the olive oil, minced garlic, chili powder, cumin, paprika, salt, and pepper. Mix well until all ingredients are evenly coated.

Heat a large skillet over medium-high heat. Add the chicken and vegetable mixture and cook for 8-10 minutes, or until the chicken is cooked through and the vegetables are tender.

While the chicken is cooking, prepare the cauliflower rice. Heat the butter or ghee in a separate skillet over medium heat. Add the grated or riced cauliflower and season with salt and pepper, to taste. Cook for 5-7 minutes, or until tender.

Serve the chicken fajitas on top of the cauliflower rice, and top with sliced avocado, shredded cheese, and fresh cilantro, if desired.

These keto chicken fajitas with cauliflower rice are a delicious and nutritious dinner option for cancer patients on a ketogenic diet. They're high in healthy fats and protein, while low in carbohydrates, making them a great choice for maintaining ketosis while nourishing your body. Plus, they're easy to customize with your favorite toppings and seasonings, so feel free to make them your own!

Baked salmon with lemon and dill

Ingredients:

- 4 salmon fillets
- 2 tbsp olive oil
- 1 lemon, thinly sliced
- 2 tbsp fresh dill, chopped
- Salt and pepper, to taste

Instructions:

Preheat your oven to 375°F (190°C). Line a baking sheet with parchment paper.

Place the salmon fillets on the prepared baking sheet. Drizzle with olive oil and season with salt and pepper, to taste.

Top each salmon fillet with a few slices of lemon and a sprinkle of fresh dill.

Bake the salmon for 12-15 minutes, or until cooked through and flaky.

Serve the baked salmon with your favorite low-carbohydrate side dishes, such as roasted vegetables or cauliflower rice.

This baked salmon with lemon and dill is a delicious and nutritious dinner option for cancer patients on a ketogenic diet. It's quick and easy to prepare, and the fresh flavors of lemon and dill add a bright, zesty kick to the dish. Plus, salmon is packed with health benefits, making it an excellent choice for supporting your overall well-being during cancer treatment.

Spaghetti squash with keto meat sauce

Ingredients:

- 1 spaghetti squash
- 1 lb ground beef or turkey
- 1/2 onion, diced
- 2 cloves garlic, minced
- 1 cup crushed tomatoes
- 2 tbsp tomato paste
- 1 tsp dried basil

- 1 tsp dried oregano
- Salt and pepper, to taste
- 2 tbsp olive oil

Optional toppings: grated parmesan cheese, chopped fresh basil

Instructions:

Preheat your oven to 375°F (190°C). Cut the spaghetti squash in half lengthwise and remove the seeds.

Brush the inside of each spaghetti squash half with olive oil, and season with salt and pepper, to taste.

Place the spaghetti squash halves cut-side down on a baking sheet and bake for 30-40 minutes, or until tender.

While the spaghetti squash is cooking, prepare the keto meat sauce. Heat the olive oil in a large skillet over medium-high heat. Add the ground beef or turkey and cook until browned and cooked through.

Add the diced onion and minced garlic to the skillet and cook until softened.

Add the crushed tomatoes, tomato paste, dried basil, and dried oregano to the skillet. Season with salt and pepper, to taste.

Simmer the sauce for 10-15 minutes, or until the flavors have melded together and the sauce has thickened.

Once the spaghetti squash is cooked, use a fork to scrape the flesh into strands.

Serve the spaghetti squash topped with the keto meat sauce, and garnish with grated parmesan cheese and chopped fresh basil, if desired.

This spaghetti squash with keto meat sauce is a satisfying and nutritious dinner option for cancer patients on a ketogenic diet. The spaghetti squash is a low-carbohydrate, nutrient-dense alternative to traditional pasta, while the keto meat sauce is packed with protein and healthy fats. Plus, it's easy to customize with your favorite toppings and seasonings, so feel free to make it your own!

Grilled Salmon with Avocado Salsa:

Ingredients:

- 4 salmon fillets

- 2 avocados, diced
- 1 small red onion, finely chopped
- 1 tomato, diced
- 1/4 cup fresh cilantro, chopped
- 2 tablespoons lime juice
- Salt and pepper to taste

Instructions:

Preheat the grill to medium-high heat.

Season salmon fillets with salt and pepper.

Grill salmon for about 4-5 minutes per side or until cooked through.

In a bowl, combine diced avocados, red onion, tomato, cilantro, lime juice, salt, and pepper to make the salsa.

Serve grilled salmon topped with avocado salsa.

Zucchini Noodles with Pesto Chicken:

Ingredients:

- 2 medium zucchinis, spiralized into noodles
- 2 boneless, skinless chicken breasts
- 1/4 cup pesto sauce (check for low-carb options)
- 1 tablespoon olive oil
- Salt and pepper to taste

Instructions:

Heat olive oil in a skillet over medium heat.

Season chicken breasts with salt and pepper and cook for about 6-7 minutes per side or until fully cooked.

Remove chicken from the skillet and slice it.

In the same skillet, add zucchini noodles and cook for 2-3 minutes until slightly softened.

Toss the zucchini noodles with pesto sauce and top with sliced chicken.

Cauliflower Crust Pizza:

Ingredients:

- 1 medium cauliflower head, riced
- 1 egg
- 1 cup shredded mozzarella cheese
- 1 teaspoon dried oregano
- 1/2 teaspoon garlic powder
- Salt and pepper to taste
- Pizza toppings of your choice (e.g., tomato sauce, cheese, pepperoni, vegetables)

Instructions:

Preheat the oven to 400°F (200°C).

Steam or microwave the riced cauliflower until tender, then squeeze out excess moisture using a clean cloth.

In a bowl, combine cauliflower, egg, 1/2 cup mozzarella, oregano, garlic powder, salt, and pepper.

Press the mixture onto a parchment-lined baking sheet to form a pizza crust shape.

Bake the crust for 15-20 minutes or until golden and crispy.

Remove from the oven, add your desired toppings, and sprinkle with the remaining mozzarella cheese.

Return to the oven and bake for an additional 10-15 minutes, until cheese is melted and bubbly.

Lemon Herb Grilled Chicken:

Ingredients:

- 4 boneless, skinless chicken breasts
- 2 tablespoons olive oil
- 2 tablespoons fresh lemon juice
- 2 cloves garlic, minced
- 1 teaspoon dried thyme
- 1 teaspoon dried rosemary
- Salt and pepper to taste

Instructions:

In a bowl, whisk together olive oil, lemon juice, minced garlic, thyme, rosemary, salt, and pepper.

Place chicken breasts in a resealable plastic bag and pour the marinade over them. Seal the bag and marinate in the refrigerator for at least 30 minutes.

Preheat the grill to medium-high heat.

Grill the chicken for about 6-7 minutes per side or until cooked through.

Spinach and Feta Stuffed Chicken:

Ingredients:

- 4 boneless, skinless chicken breasts
- 2 cups fresh spinach leaves
- 1/2 cup crumbled feta cheese
- 2 cloves garlic, minced
- 2 tablespoons olive oil
- Salt and pepper to taste

Instructions:

Preheat the oven to 375°F (190°C).

In a skillet, heat olive oil over medium heat. Add minced garlic and sauté until fragrant.

Add spinach to the skillet and cook until wilted. Remove from heat and let cool slightly.

Butterfly the chicken breasts by slicing horizontally but not all the way through.

Stuff each chicken breast with cooked spinach and crumbled feta cheese.

Secure the openings with toothpicks or kitchen twine.

Place the stuffed chicken breasts in a baking dish, season with salt and pepper, and bake for about 25-30 minutes or until cooked through.

Beef and Broccoli Stir-Fry:

Ingredients:

- 1 pound thinly sliced beef (such as sirloin or flank steak)
- 2 cups broccoli florets

- 2 tablespoons coconut aminos or low-sodium soy sauce
- 1 tablespoon olive oil
- 2 cloves garlic, minced
- 1 teaspoon ginger, minced
- Salt and pepper to taste
- Sesame seeds (optional, for garnish)

Instructions:

In a bowl, marinate sliced beef with coconut aminos (or soy sauce), minced garlic, ginger, salt, and pepper. Let it sit for 15-20 minutes.

Heat olive oil in a skillet or wok over high heat.

Add marinated beef and stir-fry for 2-3 minutes until browned. Remove from the skillet and set aside.

In the same skillet, add broccoli florets and stir-fry for 3-4 minutes until tender-crisp.

Return the beef to the skillet, toss with the broccoli, and cook for an additional 1-2 minutes.

Garnish with sesame seeds if desired and serve.

Creamy Garlic Parmesan Shrimp:

Ingredients:

- 1 pound large shrimp, peeled and deveined
- 2 tablespoons butter
- 3 cloves garlic, minced
- 1/2 cup heavy cream
- 1/4 cup grated Parmesan cheese
- 2 cups baby spinach
- Salt and pepper to taste
- Fresh parsley, chopped (for garnish)

Instructions:

In a skillet, melt butter over medium heat. Add minced garlic and sauté until fragrant.

Add shrimp to the skillet and cook for about 2 minutes per side until pink and opaque. Remove from the skillet and set aside.

In the same skillet, add heavy cream and grated Parmesan cheese. Cook, stirring, until the cheese is melted and the sauce is creamy.

Stir in baby spinach and cook until wilted.

Return the cooked shrimp to the skillet and toss to coat in the creamy sauce.

Season with salt and pepper, garnish with chopped parsley, and serve.

Eggplant Lasagna:

Ingredients:

- 1 large eggplant, sliced lengthwise into thin strips
- 1 pound ground beef or ground turkey
- 1 cup ricotta cheese
- 1/2 cup shredded mozzarella cheese
- 1/4 cup grated Parmesan cheese

- 2 cups low-carb marinara sauce
- 2 tablespoons olive oil
- 2 cloves garlic, minced
- 1 teaspoon dried basil
- 1 teaspoon dried oregano
- Salt and pepper to taste

Instructions:

Preheat the oven to 375°F (190°C).

Heat olive oil in a skillet over medium heat. Add minced garlic and sauté until fragrant.

Add ground beef or turkey to the skillet and cook until browned. Season with dried basil, dried oregano, salt, and pepper. Stir in 1 cup of marinara sauce.

In a separate bowl, mix together ricotta cheese, shredded mozzarella, and grated Parmesan.

Assemble the lasagna by layering eggplant slices, meat mixture, and cheese mixture in a baking dish.

Top with the remaining marinara sauce and a sprinkle of mozzarella cheese.

Cover the baking dish with foil and bake for 30 minutes. Remove the foil and bake for an additional 15 minutes until bubbly and golden.

Thai Coconut Curry Soup:

Ingredients:

- 1 pound boneless, skinless chicken thighs, sliced
- 2 cups cauliflower florets
- 1 red bell pepper, thinly sliced
- 1 can (14 oz) coconut milk
- 3 cups chicken broth
- 2 tablespoons Thai red curry paste
- 2 tablespoons fish sauce
- 1 tablespoon olive oil
- 1 tablespoon fresh ginger, minced
- 2 cloves garlic, minced

- Juice of 1 lime
- Fresh cilantro and sliced green onions (for garnish)

Instructions:

In a large pot, heat olive oil over medium heat. Add minced garlic and ginger and sauté until fragrant.

Add sliced chicken thighs and cook until browned.

Stir in Thai red curry paste and cook for 1-2 minutes.

Add cauliflower florets and red bell pepper slices to the pot.

Pour in coconut milk and chicken broth. Bring to a simmer and let it cook for about 15-20 minutes until the vegetables are tender.

Stir in fish sauce and lime juice.

Serve the soup hot, garnished with fresh cilantro and sliced green onions.

Greek Salad with Grilled Chicken:

Ingredients:

- 2 boneless, skinless chicken breasts

- 4 cups mixed salad greens
- 1 cucumber, sliced
- 1 cup cherry tomatoes, halved
- 1/2 red onion, thinly sliced
- 1/2 cup feta cheese, crumbled
- 1/4 cup Kalamata olives
- 2 tablespoons olive oil
- 2 tablespoons red wine vinegar
- 1 teaspoon dried oregano
- Salt and pepper to taste

Instructions:

Preheat the grill to medium-high heat.

Season chicken breasts with salt, pepper, and dried oregano. Grill for about 6-7 minutes per side or until fully cooked.

In a large bowl, combine salad greens, cucumber slices, cherry tomatoes, red onion, feta cheese, and Kalamata olives.

In a small bowl, whisk together olive oil, red wine vinegar, dried oregano, salt, and pepper to make the dressing.

Slice the grilled chicken and arrange it on top of the salad.

Drizzle the dressing over the salad and serve.

These keto-friendly dinner recipes should provide a variety of delicious and nutritious options for your cancer recipes cookbook. Remember to adapt the recipes based on dietary preferences and consult with a healthcare professional if you have specific dietary restrictions or concerns.

Chapter 5: Snack Recipes

Snacks can be an important part of a cancer patient's diet, providing an energy boost and helping to stave off hunger between meals. However, it's important to choose healthy, low-carbohydrate snacks that fit within a ketogenic diet. In this chapter, you'll find a variety of delicious and nutritious snack options, including nut and seed mixes, avocado dip with vegetable sticks, keto smoothies, and more. These snacks are easy to prepare and can be enjoyed at home or on-the-go, making them a convenient and satisfying option for cancer patients on a ketogenic diet.

Keto cheese and meat board

Ingredients:

Assorted keto-friendly meats, such as salami, prosciutto, and pepperoni

Assorted keto-friendly cheeses, such as cheddar, brie, and gouda

Olives

Nuts, such as almonds or pecans

Low-carbohydrate crackers or sliced vegetables, such as cucumber or bell pepper

Instructions:

Arrange the meats and cheeses on a large platter or board.

Add olives and nuts to the platter, filling in any empty spaces.

Serve with low-carbohydrate crackers or sliced vegetables.

This keto cheese and meat board is a satisfying and delicious snack option for cancer patients on a ketogenic diet. The combination of meats, cheeses, and nuts provides plenty of protein and healthy fats, while the low-carbohydrate crackers or vegetables add some crunch and texture. Plus, it's easy to customize with your favorite meats, cheeses, and toppings, so feel free to make it your own!

Guacamole with keto chips

Ingredients:

For the guacamole:

2 ripe avocados

1/4 cup chopped onion

1 small garlic clove, minced

1 tbsp lime juice

1 tbsp chopped fresh cilantro

Salt and pepper to taste

For the keto chips:

1 cup almond flour

1 egg

1/4 tsp garlic powder

1/4 tsp onion powder

Salt and pepper to taste

Instructions:

Preheat the oven to 350°F.

To make the guacamole, cut the avocados in half and remove the pit. Scoop the avocado flesh into a bowl and mash with a fork. Add the chopped onion, minced garlic, lime juice, chopped cilantro, salt, and pepper. Mix well and set aside.

To make the keto chips, combine the almond flour, egg, garlic powder, onion powder, salt, and pepper in a bowl. Mix well to form a dough.

Roll out the dough between two sheets of parchment paper until it's about 1/8 inch thick. Cut the dough into triangles or other desired shapes.

Place the chips on a baking sheet lined with parchment paper and bake for 8-10 minutes, or until golden brown and crispy.

Serve the guacamole with the keto chips.

This guacamole with keto chips snack is a satisfying and healthy option for cancer patients on a ketogenic diet. The guacamole provides plenty of healthy fats and nutrients, while the keto chips provide a satisfying crunch without all the carbohydrates found in traditional chips. Feel free to adjust the seasoning to your liking, and enjoy!

Keto energy balls

Ingredients:

1 cup almond flour

1/2 cup creamy peanut butter or almond butter

1/4 cup chia seeds

1/4 cup flaxseed meal

1/4 cup unsweetened shredded coconut

1/4 cup chopped nuts (such as pecans or almonds)

2 tbsp honey or a keto-friendly sweetener, such as stevia or erythritol

1 tsp vanilla extract

Pinch of salt

Instructions:

In a large mixing bowl, combine all the ingredients and mix well.

Use a cookie scoop or tablespoon to scoop the mixture and roll it into balls.

Place the energy balls on a baking sheet lined with parchment paper.

Refrigerate the energy balls for at least 30 minutes to firm up.

Store the energy balls in an airtight container in the refrigerator for up to a week. '

These keto energy balls are a tasty and nutritious snack option for cancer patients on a ketogenic diet. They're easy to make and can be customized with your favorite nuts, seeds, and keto-friendly sweeteners. Plus, they're a great way to satisfy your hunger and boost your energy levels throughout the day. Enjoy!

Deviled eggs with bacon bits

Ingredients:

6 large eggs

3 tbsp mayonnaise

1 tbsp Dijon mustard

1 tsp white vinegar

1/4 tsp salt

1/4 tsp black pepper

2 slices of cooked bacon, crumbled

Chopped chives or parsley for garnish

Instructions:

Start by boiling the eggs. Place the eggs in a pot and cover them with cold water. Bring the water to a boil, then cover the pot and remove it from the heat. Let the eggs sit in the hot water for 10-12 minutes.

Drain the hot water and transfer the eggs to a bowl of ice water. Let the eggs cool for a few minutes, then peel them.

Cut the eggs in half lengthwise and scoop out the yolks into a mixing bowl.

Add mayonnaise, Dijon mustard, white vinegar, salt, and black pepper to the mixing bowl. Mix everything together until you have a smooth mixture.

Spoon the mixture back into the egg white halves.

Top each deviled egg with crumbled bacon and chopped chives or parsley.

Refrigerate the deviled eggs for at least 30 minutes before serving.

These deviled eggs with bacon bits are a delicious and keto-friendly snack option for cancer patients on a ketogenic diet.

They're easy to make and can be prepared ahead of time, making them a great option for meal prepping. Plus, the combination of savory egg yolk filling and crispy bacon bits is sure to satisfy your cravings. Enjoy!

Avocado Deviled Eggs

Ingredients:

- 6 hard-boiled eggs
- 1 ripe avocado
- 2 tbsp mayonnaise
- 1 tsp Dijon mustard
- Salt and pepper to taste
- Paprika for garnish

Instructions:

Cut the hard-boiled eggs in half lengthwise and remove the yolks.

Mash the yolks with avocado, mayonnaise, Dijon mustard, salt, and pepper until smooth.

Spoon or pipe the mixture into the egg whites.

Sprinkle with paprika for garnish.

Chill and serve.

Zucchini Chips

Ingredients:

- 2 medium zucchinis, sliced thin
- 2 tbsp olive oil
- Salt and pepper to taste
- Optional: grated Parmesan cheese

Instructions:

Preheat oven to 225°F (110°C).

Toss zucchini slices with olive oil, salt, and pepper.

Place slices on baking sheets in a single layer.

Bake for 2-3 hours until crisp, flipping halfway through.

If desired, sprinkle with Parmesan cheese before baking.

Cool and enjoy.

Bacon-Wrapped Asparagus

Ingredients:

- 12 asparagus spears
- 6 slices bacon, cut in half
- Salt and pepper to taste

Instructions:

Preheat oven to 400°F (200°C).

Wrap each asparagus spear with a half-slice of bacon.

Place on a baking sheet and season with salt and pepper.

Bake for about 15-20 minutes or until bacon is crispy.

Serve warm.

Keto Cheese Crackers

Ingredients:

- 1 cup shredded cheddar cheese
- 1/4 cup almond flour
- 1/4 tsp garlic powder
- 1/4 tsp onion powder
- Pinch of salt

Instructions:

Preheat oven to 350°F (175°C).

In a bowl, mix shredded cheese, almond flour, garlic powder, onion powder, and salt.

Spoon small mounds of the mixture onto a baking sheet lined with parchment paper.

Flatten each mound into a thin, round cracker shape.

Bake for 8-10 minutes or until edges are golden brown.

Let cool before removing from the baking sheet.

Cucumber Cream Cheese Roll-Ups

Ingredients:

- 1 large cucumber, peeled into thin strips
- 4 oz cream cheese, softened
- 2 tbsp chopped fresh herbs (such as dill, chives, or parsley)
- Salt and pepper to taste

Instructions:

Lay cucumber strips flat on a clean surface.

In a bowl, mix softened cream cheese with chopped herbs, salt, and pepper.

Spread a thin layer of cream cheese mixture on each cucumber strip.

Roll up the cucumber strips and secure with toothpicks.

Chill in the refrigerator for about 30 minutes before serving.

Smoked Salmon Cucumber Bites

Ingredients:

- 1 English cucumber, sliced into rounds
- 4 oz smoked salmon
- 2 tbsp cream cheese
- Fresh dill for garnish

Instructions:

Place cucumber rounds on a serving platter.

Top each cucumber round with a small piece of smoked salmon.

Add a small dollop of cream cheese on top of the salmon.

Garnish with fresh dill.

Serve immediately.

Guacamole-Stuffed Cherry Tomatoes

Ingredients:

- 24 cherry tomatoes
- 1 ripe avocado, mashed
- 1 small red onion, finely chopped
- 1 small jalapeno, seeds removed and finely chopped
- 2 tbsp chopped cilantro
- Juice of 1 lime
- Salt and pepper to taste

Instructions:

Cut the tops off the cherry tomatoes and scoop out the seeds and pulp.

In a bowl, mix mashed avocado, red onion, jalapeno, cilantro, lime juice, salt, and pepper.

Spoon the guacamole into the hollowed-out cherry tomatoes.

Keto Almond Butter Fat Bombs

Ingredients:

- 1/2 cup almond butter
- 1/4 cup coconut oil, melted
- 1/4 cup unsweetened cocoa powder
- 1 tbsp powdered erythritol (or low-carb sweetener of choice)
- 1/2 tsp vanilla extract
- Pinch of salt

Instructions:

In a bowl, whisk together almond butter, melted coconut oil, cocoa powder, powdered erythritol, vanilla extract, and salt until smooth.

Spoon the mixture into silicone molds or an ice cube tray.

Freeze until firm, about 1 hour.

Pop out the fat bombs from the molds and store in the freezer.

Parmesan Crisps

Ingredients:

- 1 cup grated Parmesan cheese
- 1/2 tsp garlic powder
- 1/2 tsp dried basil
- 1/2 tsp dried oregano

Instructions:

Preheat oven to 375°F (190°C).

In a bowl, mix grated Parmesan cheese, garlic powder, dried basil, and dried oregano.

Line a baking sheet with parchment paper.

Spoon small mounds of the mixture onto the baking sheet and flatten them into thin rounds.

Bake for 5-7 minutes or until edges are golden brown and crisp.

Let cool before removing from the baking sheet.

Coconut-Lime Energy Balls

Ingredients:

- 1 cup unsweetened shredded coconut
- 1/2 cup almond flour
- 1/4 cup coconut oil, melted
- Zest and juice of 1 lime
- 2 tbsp powdered erythritol (or low-carb sweetener of choice)
- 1/2 tsp vanilla extract
- Pinch of salt

Instructions:

In a bowl, combine shredded coconut, almond flour, melted coconut oil, lime zest, lime juice, powdered erythritol, vanilla extract, and salt.

Form the mixture into small balls and place them on a plate or baking sheet lined with parchment paper.

Refrigerate for about 30 minutes to firm up before serving.

Please note that these recipes are intended for individuals following a keto diet, which is low in carbohydrates and high in fat. Adjustments may be needed based on personal dietary needs and preferences. Always consult with a healthcare professional before making significant dietary changes, especially for individuals dealing with cancer.

Chapter 6: Dessert Recipes

Desserts can be a tricky area when it comes to the keto diet, but there are still plenty of delicious options that cancer patients on a ketogenic diet can enjoy. This chapter includes a variety of keto-friendly dessert recipes that are low in carbs and sugar, but still satisfyingly sweet and indulgent.

Some examples of dessert recipes in this chapter include keto chocolate mousse, keto berry crumble, and keto cheesecake bites. These desserts use ingredients like almond flour, coconut flour, and sugar substitutes like erythritol or stevia to keep them low-carb and keto-friendly. Enjoying a keto dessert can be a great way to treat yourself while still sticking to your dietary goals.

Keto chocolate mousse

Ingredients:

- 1 cup heavy cream
- 2 tbsp unsweetened cocoa powder
- 2 tbsp powdered erythritol or stevia
- 1 tsp vanilla extract
- Pinch of salt

- Whipped cream and shaved dark chocolate for topping (optional)

Instructions:

In a mixing bowl, whip the heavy cream until it forms stiff peaks.

Add the cocoa powder, powdered erythritol or stevia, vanilla extract, and a pinch of salt to the mixing bowl. Mix everything together until you have a smooth and creamy chocolate mousse.

Spoon the chocolate mousse into dessert cups or bowls.

Chill the chocolate mousse in the refrigerator for at least 30 minutes before serving.

Top with whipped cream and shaved dark chocolate, if desired.

This keto chocolate mousse is a rich and indulgent dessert that is perfect for satisfying your sweet tooth while still sticking to your dietary goals. It's easy to make and can be prepared ahead of time, making it a great option for entertaining or meal prepping. Enjoy!

Keto pumpkin pie cheesecake

Ingredients:

For the crust:

- 1 cup almond flour
- 1/4 cup coconut flour
- 2 tbsp powdered erythritol or stevia
- 1/2 tsp cinnamon
- 1/4 tsp salt
- 1/4 cup melted butter

For the filling:

- 16 oz cream cheese, softened
- 1 cup canned pumpkin puree
- 1/2 cup powdered erythritol or stevia
- 2 tsp vanilla extract
- 2 tsp pumpkin pie spice
- 2 large eggs

Instructions:

Preheat the oven to 325°F.

In a mixing bowl, combine the almond flour, coconut flour, powdered erythritol or stevia, cinnamon, and salt. Mix everything together until it's well combined.

Pour the melted butter into the mixing bowl and stir until the mixture forms a crumbly dough.

Press the dough evenly into the bottom of a 9-inch spring form pan.

Bake the crust in the preheated oven for 12-15 minutes, until it's golden brown. Remove it from the oven and let it cool.

In a separate mixing bowl, beat the cream cheese until it's smooth and creamy.

Add the pumpkin puree, powdered erythritol or stevia, vanilla extract, and pumpkin pie spice to the mixing bowl. Mix everything together until it's well combined.

Beat in the eggs, one at a time, until the mixture is smooth and creamy.

Pour the filling over the cooled crust.

Bake the cheesecake in the preheated oven for 45-50 minutes, until the filling is set and the edges are golden brown.

Remove the cheesecake from the oven and let it cool to room temperature.

Chill the cheesecake in the refrigerator for at least 4 hours before serving.

This keto pumpkin pie cheesecake is a delicious and satisfying dessert that's perfect for any occasion. It's creamy, flavorful, and packed with warm fall spices and pumpkin flavor. Best of all, it's low-carb and keto-friendly, making it a great option for anyone on a ketogenic diet. Enjoy!

Raspberry almond flour cake

Ingredients:

- 2 cups almond flour
- 1/2 cup powdered erythritol or stevia
- 1 tsp baking powder
- 1/4 tsp salt
- 1/2 cup melted butter
- 1/2 cup unsweetened almond milk

- 2 large eggs
- 1 tsp vanilla extract
- 1 cup fresh raspberries

Instructions:

Preheat the oven to 350°F.

In a mixing bowl, combine the almond flour, powdered erythritol or stevia, baking powder, and salt. Mix everything together until it's well combined.

Pour the melted butter, almond milk, eggs, and vanilla extract into the mixing bowl. Mix everything together until it forms a smooth batter.

Pour the batter into a greased 9-inch cake pan.

Place the fresh raspberries on top of the batter, pressing them lightly into the surface.

Bake the cake in the preheated oven for 25-30 minutes, until it's golden brown and a toothpick inserted into the center comes out clean.

Remove the cake from the oven and let it cool to room temperature.

Slice the cake and serve with whipped cream, if desired.

This raspberry almond flour cake is a delicious and satisfying dessert that's perfect for any occasion. It's light, flavorful, and packed with nutritious almond flour and fresh raspberries. Best of all, it's low-carb and keto-friendly, making it a great option for anyone on a ketogenic diet. Enjoy!

Keto strawberry ice cream

Ingredients:

- 1 cup fresh strawberries
- 1 can full-fat coconut cream (13.5 oz)
- 1/2 cup powdered erythritol or stevia
- 1 tsp vanilla extract

Instructions:

Wash and hull the strawberries, then puree them in a blender or food processor until smooth.

Pour the strawberry puree into a mixing bowl and add the can of coconut cream, powdered erythritol or stevia, and vanilla extract. Mix everything together until it's well combined.

Pour the mixture into an ice cream maker and churn it according to the manufacturer's instructions, until it reaches a soft-serve consistency.

Transfer the ice cream to a container and freeze it for at least 4 hours, until it's firm.

Scoop the ice cream into bowls or cones and serve immediately.

This keto strawberry ice cream is a delicious and healthy dessert that's perfect for hot summer days or anytime you're craving something sweet. With only a few simple ingredients, it's easy to make and is a great alternative to traditional high-sugar ice cream. Enjoy!

Keto Chocolate Avocado Mousse

Ingredients:

- 2 ripe avocados, peeled and pitted
- 1/4 cup unsweetened cocoa powder
- 1/4 cup powdered erythritol or stevia

- 1 tsp vanilla extract
- Pinch of salt
- Optional toppings: whipped cream, berries, chopped nuts

Instructions:

In a food processor, blend avocados until smooth.

Add cocoa powder, sweetener, vanilla extract, and salt. Blend until well combined.

Taste and adjust sweetness if needed.

Divide into serving dishes and chill in the fridge for a few hours.

Top with whipped cream, berries, or nuts before serving.

Keto Lemon Bars

Ingredients:

- For the crust:
    - 1 1/2 cups almond flour
    - 1/4 cup powdered erythritol

- 1/4 cup melted butter
- For the filling:
  - 4 large eggs
  - 1 cup powdered erythritol
  - 1/2 cup fresh lemon juice
  - Zest of 2 lemons
  - 1/4 cup coconut flour
  - 1/2 tsp baking powder

Instructions:

Preheat the oven to 350°F (175°C) and line a baking dish with parchment paper.

In a bowl, mix almond flour, powdered erythritol, and melted butter to form the crust. Press into the baking dish and bake for 10-12 minutes, or until lightly golden.

In another bowl, whisk together eggs, powdered erythritol, lemon juice, and lemon zest.

Add coconut flour and baking powder, whisk until smooth.

Pour the filling over the baked crust and return to the oven for 20-25 minutes, until the filling is set.

Let it cool completely before cutting into bars.

Keto Berry Chia Seed Pudding

Ingredients:

- 1 cup coconut milk
- 1/4 cup chia seeds
- 1 tbsp powdered erythritol
- 1/2 tsp vanilla extract
- Mixed berries for topping

Instructions:

In a bowl, mix coconut milk, chia seeds, erythritol, and vanilla extract.

Stir well and let it sit for 10 minutes, stirring occasionally to prevent clumping.

Cover and refrigerate overnight, or for at least 4 hours, until thickened.

Serve topped with mixed berries.

Keto Coconut Macaroons

Ingredients:

- 2 cups unsweetened shredded coconut
- 1/2 cup powdered erythritol
- 3 egg whites
- 1/2 tsp vanilla extract
- Pinch of salt
- Optional: sugar-free chocolate for dipping

Instructions:

Preheat the oven to 325°F (163°C) and line a baking sheet with parchment paper.

In a bowl, mix shredded coconut, powdered erythritol, vanilla extract, and salt.

In a separate bowl, whisk the egg whites until stiff peaks form.

Gently fold the egg whites into the coconut mixture.

Use a spoon to scoop mounds of the mixture onto the baking sheet.

Bake for about 15-18 minutes, or until the macaroons are golden on the edges.

If desired, melt sugar-free chocolate and dip the bottoms of the macaroons before letting them cool.

Keto Peanut Butter Fat Bombs

Ingredients:

- 1/2 cup natural peanut butter
- 1/4 cup melted coconut oil
- 2 tbsp powdered erythritol
- 1/2 tsp vanilla extract
- Pinch of salt

Instructions:

In a bowl, mix peanut butter, melted coconut oil, powdered erythritol, vanilla extract, and salt until smooth.

Spoon the mixture into silicone molds or an ice cube tray.

Freeze for at least 2 hours, or until firm.

Pop the fat bombs out of the molds and store in the freezer.

Keto Pumpkin Spice Cheesecake Bites

Ingredients:

- For the crust:
    - 1 cup almond flour
    - 2 tbsp powdered erythritol
    - 2 tbsp melted butter
- For the filling:
    - 8 oz cream cheese, softened
    - 1/4 cup powdered erythritol
    - 1/4 cup pumpkin puree
    - 1 tsp vanilla extract
    - 1 tsp pumpkin spice blend

Instructions:

Preheat the oven to 325°F (163°C) and line a mini muffin tin with paper liners.

In a bowl, mix almond flour, powdered erythritol, and melted butter for the crust. Press into the bottom of each muffin liner.

In a separate bowl, beat cream cheese, powdered erythritol, pumpkin puree, vanilla extract, and pumpkin spice until smooth.

Spoon the filling over the crust in each liner.

Bake for about 20-25 minutes, or until the edges are set.

Let them cool before removing from the muffin tin.

Keto Chocolate Covered Strawberries

Ingredients:

- Fresh strawberries, washed and dried
- Sugar-free dark chocolate, melted

Instructions:

Line a tray or baking sheet with parchment paper.

Dip each strawberry into the melted sugar-free chocolate, letting excess drip off.

Place the dipped strawberries onto the parchment paper.

Place the tray in the refrigerator until the chocolate hardens.

Keto Vanilla Coconut Panna Cotta

Ingredients:

- 1 can (13.5 oz) full-fat coconut milk
- 1/4 cup powdered erythritol
- 1 tsp vanilla extract
- 2 tsp grass-fed gelatin
- 2 tbsp water

Instructions:

In a saucepan, heat the coconut milk and powdered erythritol over low heat until warm.

Remove from heat and stir in the vanilla extract.

In a small bowl, sprinkle gelatin over water and let it bloom for a few minutes.

Add the gelatin mixture to the warm coconut milk, stirring until dissolved.

Pour into serving glasses or ramekins.

Refrigerate for at least 2 hours, or until set.

Keto Almond Flour Brownies

Ingredients:

- 1 cup almond flour
- 1/2 cup unsweetened cocoa powder
- 1/2 cup powdered erythritol
- 1/4 tsp baking powder
- Pinch of salt
- 1/2 cup melted butter
- 2 large eggs
- 1 tsp vanilla extract

Instructions:

Preheat the oven to 350°F (175°C) and line a baking pan with parchment paper.

In a bowl, mix almond flour, cocoa powder, powdered erythritol, baking powder, and salt.

Stir in melted butter, eggs, and vanilla extract until well combined.

Pour the batter into the prepared pan and spread evenly.

Bake for 20-25 minutes, or until a toothpick inserted into the center comes out with a few crumbs.

Let the brownies cool before cutting.

Keto Cinnamon Almond Butter Bites

Ingredients:

- 1/2 cup almond butter
- 2 tbsp melted coconut oil
- 1 tsp cinnamon
- 1/4 cup powdered erythritol
- Pinch of salt
- Unsweetened shredded coconut (for coating)

Instructions:

In a bowl, mix almond butter, melted coconut oil, cinnamon, powdered erythritol, and salt until smooth.

Roll the mixture into small balls.

Roll the balls in shredded coconut to coat.

Refrigerate for at least 1 hour before serving.

These dessert recipes can be a tasty addition to a keto-focused cancer cookbook, but always make sure to consult with a healthcare professional to ensure that they align with the individual's dietary and nutritional needs during their cancer journey.

Chapter 7: Tips and Tricks for Success

Transitioning to a ketogenic diet can be a challenge, especially for cancer patients who may be dealing with additional health concerns. Here are some tips and tricks to help you succeed on a keto diet:

Start slowly: Don't try to switch to a fully ketogenic diet overnight. Gradually reduce your carbohydrate intake over the course of a week or two to give your body time to adjust.

Plan your meals: Plan your meals and snacks in advance to make sure you're getting enough healthy fats, protein, and fiber. This will help you avoid the temptation to reach for high-carb foods when you're hungry.

Stay hydrated: Drink plenty of water throughout the day to keep your body hydrated and support healthy digestion. You may also want to supplement with electrolytes, especially during the first few weeks of the diet.

Be patient: It may take a few weeks for your body to fully adapt to a ketogenic diet, so don't get discouraged if you don't see immediate results. Stick with it and be patient, and you'll start to notice the benefits.

Get support: Consider working with a healthcare professional or a registered dietitian who specializes in ketogenic diets to help you navigate the challenges and stay on track. You can also join online support groups or find a buddy who's also following a ketogenic diet for added motivation and accountability.

Meal prep ideas

Meal prep is a great way to stay on track with a ketogenic diet, especially if you're busy or short on time during the week. Here are some meal prep ideas to help you stay on track:

Roast a large batch of vegetables, such as broccoli, cauliflower, and bell peppers, and divide them into individual containers for easy reheating.

Cook a batch of protein, such as chicken breasts, ground beef, or salmon fillets, and store them in separate containers for easy meal prep. You can also make a large batch of keto meatballs or fajita meat for versatile meal options.

Prepare a large batch of cauliflower rice or zucchini noodles, and store them in individual containers for easy reheating.

Make a large batch of keto soup or chili, and store them in individual containers for a quick and easy lunch or dinner.

Make a batch of keto-friendly snacks, such as energy balls, cheese and meat boards, or deviled eggs, and store them in the fridge for a quick and easy snack option.

Pre-packaged salads with high-fat toppings like avocado and nuts can also be a great meal prep option.

Remember to keep track of your macronutrient and calorie intake to ensure you're meeting your nutritional needs and staying within your daily goals.

Grocery shopping for keto ingredients

Grocery shopping for a ketogenic diet can seem daunting at first, but with a little bit of planning, it can become second nature. Here are some tips for grocery shopping for keto ingredients:

Focus on whole, unprocessed foods: This means lots of vegetables, healthy fats, and quality protein sources.

Choose low-carb vegetables: Focus on leafy greens, cruciferous vegetables like broccoli and cauliflower, asparagus, cucumber, zucchini, and bell peppers.

Buy quality protein sources: Look for grass-fed beef, pasture-raised chicken, wild-caught fish, and organic eggs.

Choose healthy fats: Focus on avocado, coconut oil, olive oil, nuts, seeds, and fatty fish.

Avoid processed and high-carb foods: This includes sugary drinks, candy, baked goods, pasta, and bread.

Read labels carefully: Check the nutrition facts and ingredient list to ensure products are keto-friendly and don't contain added sugars or hidden carbs.

Don't forget about keto-friendly snacks: Stock up on options like nuts, cheese, olives, and jerky for when hunger strikes.

Consider meal prep: Plan your meals and make a grocery list before you go shopping to help you stay on track and avoid impulse purchases.

Remember that a ketogenic diet should be personalized to your individual needs, so adjust your grocery shopping accordingly. And don't be afraid to try new foods and recipes to keep things interesting and enjoyable!

Storing and reheating meals

Properly storing and reheating your meals is important for food safety and to ensure that your meals stay fresh and delicious.

Here are some tips for storing and reheating meals on a ketogenic diet:

Storing:

Invest in quality food storage containers: Use airtight containers that are freezer and microwave safe.

Label and date your meals: This will help you keep track of what's in your fridge or freezer and when it was made.

Store meals in the fridge for up to 3-4 days: This is the general rule of thumb for most meals. Any longer and the risk of bacterial growth increases.

Freeze meals for up to 2-3 months: This is a great option for meal prep or batch cooking. Just make sure to thaw your meals in the fridge overnight before reheating.

Reheating:

Use the microwave or oven: These are the easiest and quickest ways to reheat meals.

Add a splash of water or broth to your meals: This can help prevent your meals from drying out while reheating.

Stir frequently: This will help distribute heat evenly and prevent hot spots.

Check the temperature: Make sure your meal is heated to at least 165°F (74°C) to ensure it's safe to eat.

Consider reheating in smaller portions: This can help prevent overcooking and uneven heating.

Remember to use your best judgment when it comes to reheating meals. If something smells or looks off, it's best to throw it out and start fresh. And always be mindful of any allergies or sensitivities when storing and reheating meals.

Eating out on keto

Eating out on a ketogenic diet can be challenging, but with a little planning and knowledge, it is definitely doable.

Here are some tips for eating out on a keto diet:

Look up the menu ahead of time: Most restaurants now have their menus available online, so take a look before you go. This can help you plan your meal and make informed choices.

Stick to protein and veggies: When in doubt, go for a meal with a protein source (like meat or fish) and some non-starchy vegetables (like broccoli or green beans). Avoid foods that are high in carbohydrates, like bread, rice, or pasta.

Ask for substitutions: Many restaurants are happy to make substitutions, so don't be afraid to ask. For example, you could ask for extra veggies instead of potatoes, or a salad instead of fries.

Beware of hidden carbs: Many sauces, dressings, and marinades can be high in carbohydrates, so ask for them on the side or opt for a low-carb option like olive oil and vinegar.

Don't be afraid to customize: Many restaurants are happy to customize meals to suit your dietary needs. For example, you could ask for a burger without the bun or a sandwich on lettuce wraps instead of bread.

Avoid sugary drinks: Stick to water, unsweetened tea, or black coffee. Sugary drinks like soda, juice, or sweetened tea can quickly add up in carbohydrates.

Remember that it's okay to enjoy yourself and indulge once in a while, but if you're eating out regularly, it's important to make mindful choices to stay on track with your ketogenic diet.

Chapter 8: Conclusion

A ketogenic diet can be a valuable tool for cancer patients looking to improve their overall health and well-being. By limiting carbohydrates and increasing healthy fats and protein, a ketogenic diet has been shown to have numerous benefits, including weight loss, improved blood sugar control, and reduced inflammation.

The recipes in this cookbook are designed to provide cancer patients with delicious and satisfying meals that adhere to the principles of a ketogenic diet. With a little bit of planning and preparation, anyone can successfully follow a ketogenic diet and experience the many benefits it has to offer.

The importance of a balanced diet during cancer treatment

A balanced diet is crucial for cancer patients undergoing treatment. The body needs proper nutrition to support the immune system, repair damaged tissues, and fight infections. Cancer treatment can be physically and emotionally exhausting, and a well-balanced diet can help patients maintain their energy levels, reduce treatment-related side effects, and promote healing.

A balanced diet should include a variety of foods from all the different food groups, including fruits, vegetables, whole grains, lean proteins, and healthy fats. It is also important to stay hydrated by drinking plenty of fluids, such as water and herbal teas.

Cancer treatment can often cause side effects such as nausea, vomiting, and loss of appetite, which can make it difficult for patients to maintain a balanced diet. In such cases, it may be helpful to work with a registered dietitian who can provide guidance on how to manage these symptoms and maintain adequate nutrition.

Some cancer treatments, such as chemotherapy and radiation, can also affect the way the body absorbs and utilizes nutrients. In such cases, doctors may recommend supplements or fortified foods to ensure that patients are getting the nutrients they need.

In summary, a balanced diet is essential for cancer patients undergoing treatment. It can help support the immune system, reduce treatment-related side effects, and promote healing. Working with a registered dietitian can help patients ensure that they are getting the nutrition they need to support their overall health and well-being.

Final thoughts on the ketogenic diet and cancer

While the ketogenic diet is not a cure for cancer, it can be a valuable tool for cancer patients looking to improve their overall health and well-being during treatment. By limiting carbohydrates and increasing healthy fats and protein, a ketogenic diet has been shown to have numerous benefits, including weight loss, improved blood sugar control, and reduced inflammation.

Some studies have suggested that a ketogenic diet may also have anti-cancer properties, although more research is needed in this area. It is important to note that the ketogenic diet is not suitable for everyone, and patients should consult with their healthcare provider before making any significant dietary changes.

The recipes in this cookbook are designed to provide cancer patients with delicious and satisfying meals that adhere to the principles of a ketogenic diet. However, it is important to remember that a balanced diet that includes a variety of foods from all the different food groups is essential for overall health and well-being, particularly during cancer treatment.

Ultimately, the ketogenic diet can be a helpful tool for cancer patients, but it should be viewed as part of a larger approach to overall health and well-being. Patients should work with their healthcare provider and a registered dietitian to determine the best dietary approach for their individual needs and goals.

I would be eternally grateful if you could leave a review on Amazon if you liked learning about the Keto for cancer diet cookbook. The best way to assist your fellow readers in discovering great books is to write reviews, so do it!

Manufactured by Amazon.ca
Bolton, ON

36726593R00068